REMARKABLE PEOPLE

Katie Couric

by Erinn Banting

South Huntington Pub. Lib.
145 Pidgeon Hill Rd.
Huntington Sta., N.Y. 11746

Published by Weigl Publishers Inc.
350 5th Avenue, Suite 3304, PMB 6G
New York, NY 10118-0069

Website: www.weigl.com
Copyright ©2008 WEIGL PUBLISHERS INC.
All rights reserved. No part of this publication may be reproduced, stored in
a retrieval system, or transmitted in any form or by any means, electronic,
mechanical, photocopying, recording, or otherwise, without the prior written
permission of the publisher.

All of the Internet URLs given in the book were valid at the time of publication.
However, due to the dynamic nature of the Internet, some addresses may have
changed, or sites may have ceased to exist since publication. While the author and
publisher regret any inconvenience this may cause readers, no responsibility for
any such changes can be accepted by either the author or the publisher.

Library of Congress Cataloging-in-Publication Data

Banting, Erinn.
  Katie Couric / Erinn Banting.
     p. cm. -- (Remarkable people)
  Includes index.
  ISBN 978-1-59036-643-1 (hard cover : alk. paper) -- ISBN 978-1-59036-644-8 (soft cover : alk. paper)
  1. Couric, Katie, 1957---Juvenile literature. 2. Television personalities--United States--Biography--Juvenile literature. 3. Television news anchors--United States--Biography--Juvenile literature. I. Title.
  PN1992.4.C68B36 2008
  791.4502'8092--dc22
  [B]
                         2006039440

Printed in the United States of America
1 2 3 4 5 6 7 8 9 0   11 10 09 08 07

Editor: Leia Tait
Design: Terry Paulhus

Cover: Through her work on television, Katie Couric has shared her passion for
life and learning with millions of people.

Every reasonable effort has been made to trace ownership and to obtain
permission to reprint copyright material. The publishers would be pleased
to have any errors or omissions brought to their attention so that they may
be corrected in subsequent printings.

Contents

Who Is Katie Couric? 4
Growing Up 6
Practice Makes Perfect 8
Key Events 10
What Is a News Anchor? 12
Influences 14
Overcoming Obstacles 16
Achievements and Successes 18
Write a Biography 20
Timeline 22
Further Research 23
Words to Know/Index 24

Who Is Katie Couric?

Katie Couric is a news anchor. News anchors deliver the news on television. Katie is one of the most popular news anchors in the United States. She is well known around the world for her warm smile and friendly personality. Katie is very successful. In 2006, she was the first woman in the history of U.S. television to become the lead anchor of a major nightly news program. When she is not reporting the news, Katie works for causes she believes in. She raises money for cancer research. She helps educate people about cancer and other important issues. Katie is an important person in U.S. **culture**.

"I love being out in the field, getting the story. I feel superbly comfortable in that environment."

Remarkable People

Growing Up

Katherine Anne Couric was born on January 7, 1957. She grew up in Arlington, Virginia, with her brother, John, and her sisters, Emily and Clara. Katie's mother, Elinor, worked in the family home, raising Katie and her siblings. Katie's father, John Martin Couric, was a **journalist**. He worked for the **National Association of Broadcasters**. He was also a member of the United Press. This is a group that reports on news around the world.

In Arlington, Katie attended Jamestown Elementary school. She loved to read. One of her favorite books was *The Little Prince* by Antoine de Saint Exupéry. Another was *To Kill a Mockingbird* by Harper Lee. When she was not reading, Katie enjoyed writing. Sometimes, she wrote poetry. In school, Katie's favorite assignments were essays and book reports. In fourth grade, Katie even wrote her own newspaper.

■ Arlington, Virginia, is home to many important sites, including the Arlington National Cemetery. This is a burial place for U.S. soldiers and political figures.

6 Katie Couric

Get to Know Virginia

FLAG

INSECT
Tiger Swallowtail Butterfly

FLOWER
American Dogwood

Virginia became a state on June 25, 1788.

George Washington, the first president of the United States, was from Virginia.

More than 7 million people live in Virginia.

Richmond is the capital city of Virginia.

The northern cardinal is the official bird of Virginia. It is sometimes called the Virginia nightingale.

Think about it!

Virginia has been home to many well-known writers and journalists, such as Rita Dove, Edgar Allan Poe, and Tom Wolfe. How might this have influenced Katie when she was growing up? Think about the place where you live. Are there any local heroes who inspire you?

Remarkable People 7

Practice Makes Perfect

Katie attended middle school at Williamsburg Junior High School in Arlington. There, she pursued her love of reading and writing. These activities fueled Katie's desire to learn about people and places around the world. As she developed her writing skills, Katie knew she wanted to be a journalist, just like her father.

Katie graduated from Arlington's Yorktown High School in 1975. Later that year, she began studying English at the University of Virginia. This helped her perfect her communication skills. Katie took many courses in American studies. These classes helped her improve her knowledge of U.S. society and history.

■ The University of Virginia was founded by Thomas Jefferson. He was the third U.S president and author of the Declaration of Independence.

While in university, Katie worked for the school newspaper. It was called *The Cavalier Daily*. Katie was one of the **editors**. She helped choose stories for the paper. She also worked with writers, wrote articles, and edited the paper.

> **QUICK FACTS**
> - In high school, Katie was a cheerleader and she competed on the track team.
> - While attending the University of Virginia, Katie worked at a local radio station.
> - Katie's older sister, Emily, became a Virginia **senator** in 1995.

Katie finished her studies in 1979. She had earned a **degree** in English. After graduating, Katie began her career in journalism. In 1980, she began work at a new television network. It was called the Cable News Network (CNN). At first, she worked as a news editor. Over time, she began reporting the news. Katie worked at CNN until 1984. She spent the next few years developing her skills at many different news stations.

■ At CNN, Katie was a producer. Producers oversee all parts of a newscast. They plan news stories, write and edit scripts, and use computers to edit videotape.

Remarkable People

Key Events

In 1989, Katie married Jay Monahan. Jay was a lawyer. He sometimes appeared on television to report about legal issues. By 1989, Katie was a well-known journalist. That year, she began working for the National Broadcasting Company (NBC), now called NBC Universal. NBC was a major network. Working there was an important step for Katie.

In 1991, Katie became **co-host** of NBC's *Today* show. *Today* is a morning news and talk show. Katie hosted the show with Bryant Gumbel, and later, with Matt Lauer. She quickly became one of the most popular news anchors in the country. Katie helped make *Today* the most-watched morning show on U.S. television.

After co-hosting *Today* for 15 years, Katie made another important move. In 2006, she left *Today* to work at the Columbia Broadcasting System (CBS). Katie became the first woman to anchor the *CBS Evening News*.

■ On *Today*, Katie became good friends with her co-anchor, Matt Lauer.

Thoughts from Katie

Katie's love of learning led her to a career as a news anchor. Here are some things she has said about her life and career.

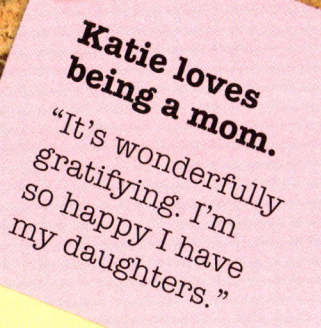

Katie thinks being a news anchor is an important job.

"I think it's really important for people to understand the issues and to make sense [of]...what's going on in our world."

Katie loves being a mom.

"It's wonderfully gratifying. I'm so happy I have my daughters."

Katie takes her job seriously.

"I've always tried to do a really good job every day, with each interview, and treat each interview seriously, and make the person I'm speaking with feel comfortable."

Katie continues to enjoy reading.

"I treasure all different kinds of books, writers, stories."

Katie moves to the *CBS Evening News* after 15 years on *Today*.

"Although it may be terrifying to get out of your comfort zone, it's also very exciting to start a new chapter in your life."

In 2006, Katie also begins working for *60 Minutes*, a current events program.

"I've always dreamed of working on that show."

Remarkable People   11

What Is a News Anchor?

A news anchor is a person who delivers the news on television, the radio, or the Internet. When two or more people present the news together, they are called co-anchors. Sometimes, television news anchors present news items live on the air, as details are fed to them on a television **prompter**. Other times, news anchors read prepared scripts. They may help write and edit these scripts. Often, the scripts are researched and written by journalists who do not appear on television.

Sometimes, news anchors such as Katie also host special programs outside of their regular news shows. Katie often hosts television specials that focus on important people or current issues in the news. Many news anchors report on special televised events, such as elections and parades, and present breaking news coverage.

■ Katie has interviewed hundreds of well-known people, including hometown heroes, world leaders, and celebrities, such as Hilary Duff.

News Anchors 101

Walter Cronkite (1916–)
Program: *CBS Evening News*
Achievements: Walter Cronkite was born in St. Joseph, Missouri. He was the first well-known U.S. television news anchor. In 1962, Cronkite became the anchor of the *CBS Evening News*. In that role, he covered many key events of the 1960s and 1970s. These included the **assassination** of President John F. Kennedy in 1963 and the first moon landing in 1969. Cronkite was so well-liked by audiences that he was often called "the most trusted man in America." He set an example for many other news anchors. After 20 years as anchor of the *CBS Evening News*, Cronkite retired in 1981.

Barbara Walters (1931–)
Programs: *Today, 20/20, The View*
Achievements: Barbara Walters was born in Boston, Massachusetts. In 1974, she became the first woman to co-anchor NBC's *Today* show. Two years later, she was the first woman to co-anchor the evening news on the American Broadcasting Company (ABC) network. Walters created a women's talk show, called *The View*, in 1997. She co-hosts the show with four other women. Walters is also well known for *The Barbara Walters Specials*, a series of interviews with celebrities and politicians. Walters is one of the most successful female news anchors in history. In 2000, she was awarded a Lifetime Achievement Award from the National Academy of Television Arts and Sciences.

Diane Sawyer (1945–)
Programs: *60 Minutes, Prime Time Live, Good Morning America*
Achievements: Diane Sawyer was born in Glasgow, Kentucky. Before becoming a news anchor, she worked as an aide, or assistant, at the White House during the 1970s. Sawyer joined CBS in 1978. She went on to host many popular programs at that network and at ABC. Sawyer is well known for her news reports and her celebrity interviews. She has won nine **Emmy Awards** for her quality news reports.

Peter Jennings (1938–2005)
Program: *World News Tonight*
Achievements: Peter Jennings was born in Toronto, Canada. His father was a well-known radio broadcaster for the Canadian Broadcasting Corporation (CBC). When he was just 9 years old, Peter began hosting his own half-hour radio show for kids. In 1964, Jennings moved to New York to work for ABC. While there, he became one of the first U.S. journalists to report from the Middle East. In 1983, Jennings became anchor of ABC's *World News Tonight*. He was the show's only anchor until his death in 2005 from lung cancer.

The Interview
An interview is a discussion used to collect information and learn the opinions of particular people, such as politicians, celebrities, and experts on certain subjects. News anchors often interview special guests while reporting the news. They question their guests about important issues and events. Some interviews are broadcast live on television. Others are taped and edited for showing at a later time.

Remarkable People

Influences

The greatest influence in Katie's life is her family. When she was a child, both of Katie's parents recognized her interest in writing. Her father encouraged her to become a journalist. He taught Katie a great deal about writing and reporting.

As an adult, Katie is inspired by her own daughters, Ellie and Carrie. When they were younger, Katie enjoyed inventing stories for them. She has published some of these stories as books so she can share them with other children. Katie's first book, *The Brand New Kid*, describes the experiences of a young boy attending a new school. The book helps teach children to be kind to one another, no matter how different they are from each other.

■ Katie's book, *The Brand New Kid*, was published in 2000.

Katie's husband, Jay, died in 1998 from colon cancer. His death made Katie want to educate people about cancer. She tells people about the disease and urges them to receive medical checkups. In 2000, Katie filmed a series of reports about colon cancer for the *Today* show. The series was called "Confronting Colon Cancer." In one report, Katie allowed her own checkup to be filmed and aired live on television. That same year, Katie helped create the National Colorectal Cancer Research Alliance (NCCRA).

■ To help raise money for cancer research, Katie often speaks at NCCRA events.

NATIONAL COLORECTAL CANCER RESEARCH ALLIANCE (NCCRA)

The National Colorectal Cancer Research Alliance is a program of the Entertainment Industry Foundation (EIF). The NCCRA was founded by the EIF, Katie, and Lilly Tartikoff, a cancer **activist**. It aims to end colon cancer by raising money for cancer research and educating people about the disease. The NCCRA funded the creation of the Jay Monahan Center for Gastrointestinal Health in New York. The center opened in 2004. It provides treatment to cancer patients and support for their families. To learn more about the NCCRA, visit **www.eifoundation.org**, and click on "National Colorectal Cancer Research Alliance."

Remarkable People

Overcoming Obstacles

Despite her success, Katie has faced obstacles in her work. Until the 1970s, very few women reported the news on television. Women journalists and reporters faced **discrimination**, and men were often awarded the top jobs. Today, most women continue to co-anchor the news with a male reporter.

Katie has never let these difficulties stop her from reaching her goals. She has strived to become a successful news anchor. Katie's hard work and dedication have helped her change history. She is the first woman in the United States to anchor the evening news without a male co-anchor.

■ Katie's first broadcast on the *CBS Evening News* took place on September 5, 2006.

Katie has overcome obstacles in her personal life. She was saddened by her husband's death in 1998. Katie felt lonely and depressed. She focused on her daughters to cope with her sadness. At the time, Ellie was six years old. Carrie was just two. Katie did her best to help her girls cope with the loss of their father. She took on the responsibilty of being a single parent. This was difficult for Katie, but it helped make her stronger.

In 2001, Katie's older sister, Emily, died of cancer. Katie misses Emily a great deal. To find comfort, she has continued her efforts to educate others and raise money for cancer research.

■ Emily Couric was a Virginia state senator for six years before her death.

Remarkable People

Achievements and Successes

Katie has received many awards during her successful career. Her top-notch reporting was first recognized in 1988. That year, Katie won an Emmy Award. She also received an award from the Associated Press. Since then, Katie has won five more Emmy Awards. In 2005, she became a member of The Academy of Television Arts and Sciences Hall of Fame.

Katie's successes go beyond her career. As a well-known news anchor, Katie educates and influences the world. By allowing her medical checkup to be filmed and broadcast on television, Katie influenced 20 percent more people in the United States to receive medical checkups for colon cancer. As a result, Katie won the George Foster Peabody Award in 2001. This award recognizes excellence in broadcasting.

- In 2004, Katie was a presenter at the *Glamour* magazine Women of the Year Awards. Two years later, she received one of these awards for her work with the EIF.

More women currently anchor news programs and work behind the scenes than ever before. They make important decisions and ensure that networks report news that matters to both men and women. Katie is one of these women. She has been a **role model** for many women in U.S. television news. Her achievements have made it easier for other women to enter the field. Katie has won two Gracie Allen Awards from the Foundation of American Women in Radio and Television. These awards honor her achievements on behalf of women in television news.

Katie draws attention to women's and children's issues around the world. She is an **ambassador** for the United Nations Children's Fund (UNICEF). On behalf of the group, Katie visited children in Zimbabwe in 1992. She often urges viewers to become involved in UNICEF programs. In 2003, Katie received UNICEF's Danny Kaye Humanitarian Award for her work in the interest of women and children.

THE UNITED NATIONS CHILDREN'S FUND (UNICEF)

UNICEF is a group that works to improve life for children around the world. The group was created in 1946. It is run by the United Nations, an organization made up of many countries. UNICEF aims to protect children and children's rights across the globe. Its programs focus on health care, nutrition, and education for all children. UNICEF works in more than 190 countries to improve life for the world's children. To learn more about UNICEF, visit the group's youth website at **www.unicef.org/voy**.

Remarkable People

Write a Biography

A person's life story can be the subject of a book. This kind of book is called a biography. Biographies describe the lives of remarkable people, such as those who have achieved great success or have done important things to help others. These people may be alive today or they may have lived many years ago. Reading a biography can help you learn more about a remarkable person.

At school, you might be asked to write a biography. First, decide who you want to write about. You can choose a news anchor, such as Katie Couric, or any other person you find interesting. Then, find out if your library has any books about this person. Learn as much as you can about him or her. Write down the key events in this person's life. What was this person's childhood like? What has he or she accomplished? What are his or her goals? What makes this person special or unusual?

A concept web is a useful research tool. Read the questions in the following concept web. Answer the questions in your notebook. Your answers will help you write your biography.

Katie Couric

WRITING A BIOGRAPHY

Your Opinion
- What did you learn from the books you read in your research?
- Would you suggest these books to others?
- Was anything missing from these books?

Childhood
- Where and when was this person born?
- Describe his or her parents, siblings, and friends.
- Did this person grow up in unusual circumstances?

Adulthood
- Where does this individual currently reside?
- Does he or she have a family?

Main Accomplishments
- What is this person's life's work?
- Has he or she received awards or recognition for accomplishments?
- How have this person's accomplishments served others?

Work and Preparation
- What was this person's education?
- What was his or her work experience?
- How does this person work; what is or was the process he or she uses or used?

Help and Obstacles
- Did this individual have a positive attitude?
- Did he or she receive help from others?
- Did this person have a **mentor**?
- Did this person face any hardships?
- If so, how were the hardships overcome?

Remarkable People 21

Timeline

YEAR	KATIE COURIC	WORLD EVENTS
1957	Katie is born on January 7.	Dwight D. Eisenhower begins his second term as president of the United States on January 21.
1980	CNN firsts broadcasts on June 1. Katie begins working at the new network.	Black Entertainment Television (BET) launches on January 25.
1989	In July, Katie becomes a correspondent for NBC. That same year, she marries lawyer Jay Monahan.	The satellite television service, Sky Television plc, is launched in Europe in February.
1991	On April 5, Katie becomes co-host of NBC's *Today* show.	British scientist Tim Berners-Lee launches the World Wide Web on August 6.
1998	Katie's husband Jay dies of colon cancer in January.	The British Broadcasting Corporation (BBC) launches BBC America in the United States on March 29.
2000	Katie helps found the NCCRA. In March, she films a special report on colon cancer.	News anchors around the world host celebrations to mark the beginning of the next 1,000 years on January 1.
2006	On September 5, Katie becomes anchor of the *CBS Evening News*.	UNICEF celebrates its 60th anniversary.

Further Research

How can I find out more about Katie Couric?

Most libraries have computers that connect to a database for searching for information. If you input a key word, you will be provided with a list of books in the library that contain information on that topic. Non-fiction books are arranged numerically, using their call number. Fiction books are organized alphabetically by the author's last name.

Websites

To learn more about Katie Couric, visit
www.cbsnews.com
> Click on "CBS Evening News" and then on "Bios" to access Katie's biography.

To learn more about journalism, visit
www.writesite.org/html/newsroom.html

Remarkable People 23

Words to Know

activist: a person who works for a cause
ambassador: an official representative
assassination: the murder of someone for political reasons
co-host: someone who serves as master of ceremonies of a television program or event with someone else
culture: the arts, beliefs, and social practices that make up a group's way of life
degree: a title given to a student by a college, university, or professional school after completion of his or her studies
discrimination: treating people unfairly for improper reasons, such as their gender or race
editors: people who obtain and improve the content of a book, magazine, or newspaper
Emmy Awards: awards given each year by the National Academy of Television Arts and Sciences for excellence in television
journalist: someone who writes news stories
mentor: a wise and trusted teacher
National Association of Broadcasters: an association that works on behalf of radio and television stations as well as broadcast networks
prompter: a device that displays words for people to read
role model: a person whom others admire
senator: a member of the senate, a branch of government that makes laws

Index

American Broadcasting Company (ABC) 13
awards 18, 19
Brand New Kid, The 14
Cable News Network (CNN) 9, 22
CBS Evening News 10, 11, 13, 16, 22, 23
Columbia Broadcasting System (CBS) 10, 13
Couric, Emily 6, 9, 17
Couric, John Martin 6, 14
Cronkite, Walter 13
interviews 11, 12, 13
Jay Monahan Center for Gastrointestinal Health 15
Jennings, Peter 13
Monahan, Jay 10, 15, 17, 22
National Assocation of Broadcasters 6
National Broadcasting Company (NBC) 10, 13, 22
National Colorectal Cancer Research Alliance (NCCRA) 15, 22
news anchors 4, 10, 11, 12, 13, 16, 18, 19, 22
Sawyer, Diane 13
Today 10, 11, 13, 15, 22
United Nations Children's Fund (UNICEF) 19, 22
University of Virginia 8, 9
Virginia 6, 7, 8, 9, 17
Walters, Barbara 13
women's issues 19

FEB 16 2010
2445